AF434202

I'm not a poet

I'm not a poet

a poetry
collection

Suleiman Adeyemi

Minhaj Publicity

Reviews

Suleiman Adeyemi's I'm not a poet is a playful invitation to consider the validity of its premise, while ultimately asking readers to consider more deeply the line between what each of us may or may not consider art, or it's creator an artist (this certainly SEEMS like poetry, doesn't that make him a poet?).

And yet, as the playful, humorous, and self-deprecating work in Part 1 evolves into the richer, more mature pieces in Part 2 and beyond, there's no longer any question - this is poetry. Along with this shift, the self-doubt expressed in the title dissolves too, as if we are witness to Adeyemi further embracing his poetic identity in real time with each further poem and with each turn of the page. The overall structure of the collection suggests the story of a young man initially in doubt of this label "poet", but who embraces this identity more and more though habitually processing his thoughts, goals, and life experiences (about love, xenophobia, becoming a teacher, and Philadelphia, for instance) through poetic reflection.

And what we're ultimately left with is a thought-provoking, beautifully written and structured, and often smile-inducing poetic memoir, by an inciteful author with a creative spirit and an imaginative and artistic way with words. By a poet.

Dale Placek
Doctoral Candidate
University of Maryland, College Park
Department of Teaching and Learning, Policy and Leadership

#2

A fine contribution to the rising tide of authenticity flowing from the next generation of thinkers and leaders.

Dr. Daniel J. Collins-Cavanaugh
Professor of Philosophy

#3

Suleiman Adeyemi presents a fresh new voice to the world of poetry. He provides a cross section of thought provoking, soul searching verses that reflects life on many levels. As an 82- year-old senior citizen, I can relate to the themes that this young man has portrayed in verse. And those who are in various stages of life can reflect on their past and explore their future through his words.

The poignant verses referenced from the following two poems:

> *Why I Write:* "I write so I could pretend to be a poet
> So, friends could think me intelligent."

> and

> *This Is Poetry:* "My gaze starts with a puzzle,
> But ends in a smile."

As you prepare to become engaged, immersed, and inspired by Suleiman's poetry, you will soon agree that he is not a *"pretend poet"*; and some of his verses intrigue the *"puzzled mind,"* but make us *"smile."*

Suleiman is the "intelligent" real deal—a real poet.

Mae Askew
Associate Professor of English

ISBN: 978-978-991-264-3

Minhaj Publicity

44 Adesuwa Road, GRA, Benin City
Edo State, Nigeria

6490 Landover Rd, Suite C5
Hyattsville, MD, 20785

www.minhajpublicity.com | minhajpublicity@gmail.com

Dedication

To the three women in my life, the one who brought me to the world and the two who came after me.

Contents

III

IV

V

VI

VII

VIII

IX

Foreword

Over the years, poetry has played memorable roles in the world. It has shaped generations of scholars, leaders, masses, etc. It is irrefutable that poetry, as oldest as earth, has also been a crucial tool in the hands of people who invest critically in deploying it as a mirror, or as a seer to peer into the future. This realization has taught us that despite the terrible things happening in the world, we could find repose in words, in lines and verses of poems that paint our fears and assure us of better years ahead.

Following the traditions of poetic ancestors and torchbearers whose ideas of poetry rendered the world safe to live, Suleiman offers us, in this terrific debut poetry collection, a window through which we can gaze endlessly at the sky laden with words, dressed in the garb of stories birthed by life and the persona's experiences. As a reader, it is important to listen to these words hum on pages, their slim bodies twisting in your palm each time you hold them.

It is a digital world. In recent times, poetry has continued to gain traction on digital platforms. This has shaped the ways we critically engage it, as it opens portals of interpretations to those who invest in unravelling its intricacies, its endless network of meanings and ideas. However, Suleiman's poetry, as far as I know, does not reflect the everydayness of poetic language used on social media platforms. His ability to detail life changing experiences and to show us, through simple but thought-provoking verses the essence of life, is noteworthy.

In each poem, the reader voyages through the fluidity of lines. Sometimes written with the use of a rhyme scheme, Suleiman pays homage to the master poets through his deployment of this distinct style of conveying his thoughts and ideas to us. Some of the poems in this collection portray life as ordinary, while other poems about poetry identify with its significance in our society.

In a poem titled "This is poetry," he reinforces the indescribable power of poetry and the mystery surrounding this genre of literature that astounds us endlessly. He writes:

> In front of me are words
> I wish were mine
> These stanzas are like murals
> painted on a wall
> Every line has me
> asking for more
> The imagery is vivid
> Its words, concrete
> Its meter is specific
> And message, authentic (19)

This poem, and others in this collection, celebrate poetry in its pristine form. Suleiman also attests to the quotidian celebration of love in our lives. In his love poems, he piques our minds with soothing verses and also addresses his love with honeyed lines. This aspect of the poet's collection accentuates what most poets do in their engagement of love. In "I thank you," he writes:

> People say I have a way with words
> But since I saw you,
> I've been lost for words
> If I was given a pen and paper
> to come up with a perfect wife,
> I couldn't draw a picture as perfect as you
> You're not beautiful
> You are beauty (72)

The celebration of the beauty resonates in some of the poems in this collection. The essence of poetry is defined, and Suleiman allows us to relish each poem through his masterful handling of diction. This linguistic mastery is also evident in other poems in the collection.

Dear reader, here I leave you to enjoy yourself. Also, always remember this: that the poet has come with his own voice and songs. Let's listen!

Rasaq Malik
Ìbàdàn
25/6/2021

I

Poetry

Why I write

I write:
So, I could pretend to be a poet
So, friends could think me intelligent
Because I'm not the best talker
And words on paper don't stutter

I write:
Because writing affords me more time
To feign eloquence with dumb rhymes
As I give life to meaningless lines
With run-ons begging for punctuation marks

I write:
Because I've been told I'm good at it
And it gives me a reason to be happy
As I collect the trash that life throws at me
And litter my pages with it.

I wish

I wish I wrote a piece
so sublime,
that is rich without a dime,
flows without a rhyme,
and stands the test of time.

I wish I wrote a piece
that compels the young
and reminds the old,
inspires the weak
and humbles the bold.

I wish I wrote a piece
with thoughts the eye can see,
words that tickle your fancy,
and a message that lives after me.
A piece, bigger than me.

This is poetry

My gaze starts with a puzzle
but ends in a smile
In front of me are words
I wish were mine
These stanzas are like murals
painted on a wall
Every line has me
asking for more
The imagery is vivid
Its words, concrete
Its meter is specific
And message, authentic
I had to think about its language
Not for its ambiguity
But in appreciation of its beauty
It speaks a dialect I understand
Said so much with so little
This is poetry, personified.

Is this poetry? (or Untitled)

There I was in my queen-size bed
laying down in my 14-by-12 room.
The sound of the AC breaks its silence.
Pieces of dirty cloth, crumbs of dry bread,
and pairs of smelly shoes littered the room.
The whiff of egusi reeked within.
There I was laying innocently
oblivious of the mess around me.
Wools from the bedsheet
tangled with a few strands of my scruffy
but wavy hair like a tug of war as I toss and turn.
It would be difficult to choose
what was messier between myself and my room.
GRIN-GRIN, GRIN-GRIN, GRIN-GRIN…
At 4:30, my phone alarm rang through the room
and brought me back to reality.
I patted my bed back and forth
searching for the gadget and desperately
hoping to click on snooze.
I was too tired to wake up at the time,
so I snoozed the alarm to 04:40,
but I woke up at 5:20.

Poets are liars

A poem with too many rhymes is probably a lie
I promise you poetry is nothing hard to do
You could write a piece of baloney
and call it a poem too
Poets are naked emperors
and you all are sycophantic listeners
You pat their backs;
now to your praises they are prisoners
They spend hours writing profound pieces
with no meanings
At the end, poetry is another lie
that sometimes says the truth

This or those

I know I suck at grammar
So, I hide behind poetic license
I could have excelled in drama
But I'm a bad liar

I'm amazed by art
So, it's either ink on a page
Or paints on canvas...
I wrote two stanzas

Poetic Justice

You can't be serious, lady!
How can you call this poem amazing?
It's like a fake version of a bad prose
Even with its rhymes it lacks flows

Am I too dumb to see its beauty?
Is it saying something truly?
Do I need spectacles to see its spectacle?
Is this some sort of peekaboo?

This can't be for a baby boomer
And its audience can't be woke
If the piece is a funny attempt at humor
Congratulations: the piece is a joke.

Maybe this poem is not corny
And I'm just a jealous dummy
I would love the benefit of the doubt
But Nah! This poem does reek of crap

II

Compass

Hope

I've seen the earth
throw my filth right at me
I've smiled at life,
and it laughed back at me

I've found success
in things I didn't understand
I've known failure
like the back of my hand

I've tasted defeat:
raw and cold
I've dug my own grave
looking for gold

I've seen kindness
mistaken for weakness
I've seen love
pronounced sickness

I've encountered men
who cause pain for wit
Not for fame,
status, or profit

I've known misery
and its battalion
I've heard of victory
and its companion

I've faced life
with fine plans
But that rascal
beats me with its pranks

But I never
lose hope
I don't tie that renegade
with a loose rope.

You can win

Your dreams are too big for your sleep
So, have them while awake

You can be a star
If you stay up at night

You can move mountains
If you keep your feet on the ground

You can touch the sky
If you learn how to fly

You can win
If only you try

Song & dance

I fell too many times
Why rise again?
Why stay in the fight?
When pity only comes with pain

I could run out of will not excuses,
I could blame my raggy gloves,
The battlefield with saggy turves,
The foes in the mocking crowd,
The friends who failed to cheer aloud,
The gloom of the pregnant cloud,
The rain that wet the soil,
The boot for the slippery toil,
My adversary for being rough,
And time for calling my bluff.
I could hue and cry,
And curse the evil eye.
I could blame everything but me.

Or

I could rise up
and look within.
And be the brave coward
that refused to give in

Tomorrow owes you nothing

Before you aim to conquer the world, big
Can you clean up your home, at least?
You long for what the future brings
While you have the present within reach

The dead victories of yesterday
Can't save you in the wars of today
Don't wonder about tomorrow in awe
If you have not conquered today at all

If you are patient with today's plight
Tomorrow should bring a better sight
So, if you give today all you've got,
Tomorrow might pay you back

The enemy

I woke up knowing time isn't on my side
To survive, I must strive against the tide

The day isn't meant for sleep but trials
Don't be a sheep in the midst of lions

Laugh a little because life isn't a play
And cry less for sunlight is a night away

You'd meet failure on your way to the top
Just keep climbing and never think to stop

Victory could come in a different gown
Learn about it forms before it skips town

Your greatest enemy is in the mirror
But breaking the glass won't kill the figure

So, conquer the battles in you
Because the enemies outside are few.

Oh tears!

Oh tears!

Can you wash away my sorrow?
Can you quench this pang of pain?
Or would my worries
leave a mark on my soul as you on my face?
I hope my peace is not as rare as you
I hope my dreams are as real as you
I hope my burdens fall off as you drop
I feel pain when I cry
I see hope as you dry
As you water the dirt beneath me
Let my dreams blossom into reality.

Dreams

You went to bed without your glasses
How do you see in your dreams?

Even with your visions
Tomorrow is blurry
Actually, the future is scary
Age has given me a glimpse
Into the reality of dreams
Life isn't always what it seems
I despise the devil and his schemes
As I lose the battle against my whims
Life can be sweet like honey
yet sting like bees

Honey!
It's not a game so give your all
It's not a shame if you fall
So, rise again, again, and again
Fight till you can't throw any other punch
Use the rope as a crutch
Don't bite your way out of a clutch
This truth is bitter
So, I spit it while you sleep
But I hope it finds its way
into your dreams

Until then,
Have your dreams the old way
And wake up to a new day.

I know tales

I know tales of men who have tasted victory
Stories with failure as an accessory
Show me a mogul who's paid no cost
How can you be said a winner if you've never lost?

It was said that every tale has a silver lining
But no one wants to tell stories with no sweet ending
To succeed is to fail in giving up
How beautiful is success with no failure in its makeup?

Black & white

You walked through the black and white gate
I sat on a fence painted grey
For not all doors are meant to be crossed
As not all puzzles are meant to be solved

Not all questions have a reply
Sometimes you can't tell a truth from the lie
Sometimes you don't know the "why"
And to move forward, you must stand by

When the bees pour out of their hive
And the wind and dust connive
To bury you alive
Staying still is how you survive

When you become a king

When you become a king
and the world's beneath your feet

But your jewelry feels like shackles
and your apparel like rags and tatters

When your palace seems like a prison
and your crown just another burden

When tomorrow seems like a million miles
and tears sought shades behind your smiles

Just cry out and pray to your lord
For tears are sadness beyond words

I was not made

I was not made to be a spectator
My sweat and blood must leave a trail
I will fight through as a gladiator
And cherish my bruises even if I fail

I was not made to live for greed
For there are blessings in giving
I will answer every call of need
For charity is an act relieving

I was not made for life to rest
I will work till my muscles strain
As my fist hits the wall of tests
There's joy behind every pain

I was not made to beg or ask
For there is dignity in self-reliance
I will rise up to the task
Savoring the toils of independence

I was made to make a mark
With my being and struggle
Every fire begins with a spark
Every effort is worth the trouble

These little things

Happiness resides in...

the warmth of a mother's smile
after a child's favor worth a while,

a coin wrapped in the beggar's palm
as a gift from the stranger in town,

the yawn that beckons a new day
after a night of dreams tucked away,

and the contentment of the soul
as you appreciate your own.

Unnoticed by distracted beings,
happiness resides in these little things.

Life's lessons

Lesson I:
Life is a battle,
and you are a soldier abroad
Get your hands dirty,
and strike your boot to the mud
Pray to your Lord
if you can no longer hold the sword
Victory tastes sweeter
if you succeed against the odd

Lesson II:
The past is lost in the ruins of time,
so it's not worth much
Your memories are a lesson,
so treat them as such
Firmly hold them loose
and never lose your touch
To conquer the world,
use your beginnings as a crutch

Lesson III:
Protect your good tidings:
beware of envy
Life goes in circle,
so walk the earth gently
Your allies are your mirrors,
so choose them wisely

Be friends with a few,
but with most be friendly

Lesson IV:
If you must be a hero,
be unsung
Men singing your praises
are probably wrong
You know you,
so keep your head strong
Never pay your mind
to a lying tongue

Lesson V:
A dirge is not without melody,
so, never live for men's eulogy
Silence is not gold
if the truth goes untold
So, if a lie and the truth
ever pick a fight
Be with the truth,
for you must pick a side

Think!

Walk the earth with your shoulders high
But you will never touch the sky
Own everything money can ever buy
But you can't afford an eye

Makes me wonder why
You think yourself so high
But as time goes by and by
Think! What happens after you die?

May your days be wild

May your days be wild
For victory is not for the mild

Never ignore the clock and its chime
For a filled up day gives wings to time

Always trade boredom for hectic
A glorious path's not for the lethargic

You would be accompanied by troubles
Your journey would be filled with wobbles

Life, like a thief, would steal your earnings
And shove you back to your humble beginnings

But if you persevere
Victory lies in a future, near.

III

Living every day

Educere

I know you don't want to pay the price
But because the truth is expensive
I won't sell you lies
A word, they say, is enough for the wise
I don't think you're dumb
I won't say it twice

Kids are books authored by society
The first few chapters are written by the family
Before you inscribe that ink on the scrolls
You should know you oversee what the future holds

Your eyes are his sight
Your strengths are his might
Your beliefs become his actions
Your habits are his addictions

A boy dreams what a man does
Your inaction is your child's loss
Give him peace but show him war
His safety, you won't always be responsible for

Nobody knows tomorrow
The future could be a curse
Take him away from sorrow
but get him set for the worst
Give kids knowledge so diverse
That they would find their way

no matter what path they traverse

He needs the love of a mother
Because the nanny can't be another
Give him the courage of a father
And his mind will not falter

Why use your tongue
when your actions can communicate
For that is easier to emulate
He can by himself educate
But his freedom,
you must regulate

Raise him on a farm
he would be a farmer
Take him to the market
and you'd mold a merchant
But how can you play your part
if you don't know what it is?
How should they deal with hardship
if all they've known is ease?

I know you don't want to pay the price
But because the truth is expensive
I won't sell you lies
A word, they say, is enough for the wise
I don't think you're dumb
I won't say it twice

I've learned

Teaching is an art, anyone can learn
I know I have the heart, my passion is no concern
But if you want to teach, you always have to learn
Like never give a fish when I could teach how to earn
A living. And that's something I've learned.

You know, I came in as a boy now I feel like a man
Never use to like kids, but now I'm a fan
I've learned to think ahead, thanks to lesson plan
I've learned to make a guess of what the kids could say
The answers they might give, the questions they could raise
When things don't go as planned, I'll make it work anyways

I've grown in confidence, could look you straight in your face
Plus, I know my voice has a good base
But when it comes to talk, I have to slow down my pace
And stop speaking as though I'm in a race
You do good, I praise. You do bad, I reprimand
Your full attention that's all I demand

I've learned so many things. I got better a notch
Like how to interact, kids you shouldn't touch,
Should have a wait time, never never never rush
But try to stick to the time, I need to buy me a watch
And speaking of patience, I need that a bunch
I mean how do you deal with kids that make a mess of their lunch

I've learned new terms like "turn and talk,"
"Exit tickets," "common core"
Yes, I've learned. I've grown
I'm not done. I know
I'm working on talking slow
I'm
Working
On
Talking
Slow

I want to play my part. I want to make a mark
I want to be the light that will take you out of the dark
I'm not going to hold your hands. I'm just going to guide you
And if you don't want to learn. I won't even mind you
You came here to learn. I'm going to remind you
I'll try my best to excite you

Never be deceived. There's nothing that you can't do
I will make you discuss with the kid you are next to
When you get stuck, we would come to your rescue
And after every lesson, I'm going to test you
I know you don't like it, but I want to make you the best you
When you see your grades, the best view
When your C's turn A's, successful

I'm going to get you involved
I'm going to call you by names
Wake you up from your sleep
I'm going to bring up the flames

Class objective is the first on my page
I want to know what you know: I want to engage
Before I explain, we're going to explore
Then, we conclude.

Alas!

Alas!
It was the first day of class
So, I came early. I didn't want to take last
Chilling in my black skin, I got kufi on my wavy hair
No one sitting next to me, but I really do not care
Oh! I think I know. Maybe it's my accent
Although in reading, I'm fervent
I got a library in my apartment
I speak three languages: I'm learning a fourth
They don't even know the kind of battles I fought
Yes, I sleep little, but I dream big
I trash my sorrow like a bad wig

Now let's go back to class!
It's time for attendance
The first name was Adan, Douglass
The professor said it with a smile
My name comes next, so she wished she could pass
But the lady had to play nice, so she asked,
"How do you say your name?"
"SOO-LAY-MAN," I replied
She couldn't say it even though she tried
Now I'm feeling bad
Is my name so freaking hard?
"Can I call you by a nickname?" she requested
"You can call me Ade," I suggested.

I wasn't even disappointed.
Because while the students laugh at my accent in shame
The professor couldn't even pronounce my name

IV

Catching flies

Dear cousin,

Cousin!
I pray you grow up being wise
If you turn out dumb,
I plead that you study hard
If you refuse to study hard,
I implore you not to waste your time
If you must waste your time,
I urge you not to spend it on TV
If you will watch TV,
I beg that you stay away from sport
If you must follow sport,
I beseech you don't choose soccer
If you must watch soccer,
I hope you don't support a team
If you must be loyal to a team,
I pray,
I plead,
I implore,
I urge,
I beg,
I beseech,
and I hope
it's not Arsenal Football Club.

What does she mean?

"Is his future bright?"
She asked
"How?" I probed

Does she mean like
the moon that lights up her earth
Or a candle at the mercy of her breath?

Does she mean like
A lantern that accentuates her face
Or a bulb that illuminates her space?

Does she mean like
The sun that brightens her day
Or a lamp that kindles her way?

Does she mean like
A fire that ignites her passion
Or the torch that aids her vision?

What does she mean?
She must pick one
I can't be all the above.

Scaredy-cat

I thought it was rain beating on my roof
or footsteps squeezing their way
through the cracks on my wall

I looked out the window
but the cloud was clear
I scouted the street;
no foot was near

Then, I wondered
what sound is it
that rises at night
and sleeps at dawn?

For sounds don't make themselves.
There's a dog behind a bark,
a cat behind a meow,
and a mouse behind
whatever sounds they make.

My neighbor owns a dog,
but I never heard it bark.
And I am pretty sure
I know the meow of a cat.

So, crazy mouse
Whatever place you are...
You creepy nocturnal
and dark feces secreting devil.
Scurry your pointed snout
and long tail out of my home.

I must warn you!
I am a cat,
a scaredy one.

V

Purpose

The man

He (May peace be upon him) was a man
But his message was divine
He couldn't read or write
But came with a message that's nothing alike
You must be deaf, dumb, and blind
To deny the message of a man.
That went to the heavens and came back in one
Night

He could have been the king but chose to be a slave
He came to teach us how to behave
To worship Allah not some bones in the grave
Peace be upon the man whose name stems from praise
A man whose status was raised
He came with a message for the past, the future, and today
I don't care what the haters say
I just hear and obey

Do & die

Life isn't do or die
Life is do & die
Could be a thin line
between truth and lie
Between you and I
you know we live to die

I'm a Muslim
I will die to live
Life is a battle
I need to pull up my sleeve
My last breath, a sigh of relief
I will not die if I believe

"Every soul shall taste death. And only on the Day of Ressurection shall you be paid your wages in full" (Qur'an 3:185).

VI

Match and gasoline

To my future wife

To my future wife,
I don't care where you're from
You could be
Pakistani, Somali,
Bengali, from Mali
I find beauty in all people
I'm not racist
And before I forget
Nigeria...that's where my base is
But don't be scared
I'm not a fake prince
Yes! I know about the stereotypes
but I'm not that type
When it comes to the deen
I follow the lead
of Abu Bakr, Umar, Uthman, and Ali

I study books like Usool uth-thalatha and Kitab At-Tawhid
But I'm still working on my tajwid
I love the collection of An-Nawawi
I'm a big fan of sheikh Al Albani
To be honest, I prefer to go by Salafi
But I know people got beef with that title, so you can call me Sunni
I'm not a Sufi. I occasionally don a kufi
I got my pants above the ankles: I try to follow the sunnah straight
And if you give me a chance, I would love to illustrate

I'm not sure if my goatee count as a beard
But I never shaved it. This was how it appeared
When it comes to food, I'm completely weird
I'm a picky eater
I don't eat pizza
I play too much, plus I'm a deep sleeper
All I'm saying is…
I'm not perfect and neither are you
All I need is a Muslimah on deen
She covers complete. She looks like a queen
She's chaste and protects what's in between
She goes without makeup because beauty is from within
She lowers her gaze because shyness is from the deen
She prays and does her fast
And definitely the coolness of my eyes
So, if you think you're the one for me
My name is Suleiman
I'd like to meet your walee

My world

She means the world to me, literally
So, I love her stereotypically
Her complexity transcends
a place, time, or ethnicity

She's traversed so many paths
But I could navigate her train of thoughts
She's innocent
I don't mind her faults

For her, I have patience
I will take her nonsense
That's how much she means to me...
My world

My feelings don't lie

I'm not one of those fools
that loves someone but don't know why
I love you
and the reasons are not hard to find
I know exactly why
I can't get you off my mind
I don't think you're one in a million
I think you're one of a kind
It took me years to find you
I have a lot of things to write about you
How just the thought of you
makes me smile
How you look beautiful
even when you cry
This is what I feel
and my feelings don't lie

I thank you

People say I have a way with words
But since I saw you,
I've been lost for words
If I was given a pen and paper
to come up with a perfect wife,
I couldn't draw a picture as perfect as you
You're not beautiful
You are beauty
But it's not about the looks
It is not about the looks
A tale like ours
can only be found in books
I did 95 on 95
just to see you
And when I did
you're 10 over 10
You're amazing
you're wonderful
You're like a star on a stage
You're wise beyond your age
You're calm, bold, shy, smart
Jealous, religious
Precious, ambitious
You got class
You're classy
SubhanAllahi

I can't believe I found you
Would you really give me a chance
to spend the rest of my life around you?
Would you?
If so,
I'm blessed,
I'm grateful,
and I thank you

Love blinds

He knows
what to do with her
He gave a rose
because flowers do wither

Love is a fight, so like gloves
I see the ring
on the hand of the bride
And one eyed will be the king
in the land of the blind

Some think love is a play
like "Romeo and Juliet"
But it's "Arms and the Man"
so get your arrows and bullet

I see the arrow and the stain
I see the sorrow and the pain
I see the hollow in her gain
I see the marrow and her vein

Cupid:
worshipped by the Romans
Stupid:
he gossips about her romance

She could give him her life
but life is priceless
But he can't give her his heart
though that cost less

There is no harm in testing
so she gave it a try
But her heart is broken
so is her thigh

He said he loved her,
but he lied
He said just her,
but he had nine

So please trust nobody
emotions do lie
Love is bloody
feelings do die

Can I write you a poem?

Can I write you a poem?
Can I screenshot you on a page?
Can I make you a star on my stage?
I promise I will give it all it takes
I will precisely choose words with no mistakes
I will literally make a copy with no hyperbole
I will rhyme you into reality
Like a gift,
I will present you to the world
I will wrap you in nice words
I will make you a masterpiece
So, please!
Let me write you a poem.

I can love you but…

I can love you, but
you must know first
That loving you
comes with a cost

You must love me
with everything you got
I tend to forget,
so you must remind me a lot

And you must be
capable of being loved
Can you handle this
my beloved?

VII

Playing one's part

Peace out!

News can shatter
like a mirror
when it's broken
And words can be sharper
than a sword
when they're spoken
But I won't break my word
For I'm a brave coward
I'm a slave outward
I'm scared but not fleeing
Because I gave my word
Because I gave my word

I have a lot to say,
a lot to write home about
Because sometimes life in this place
Is nothing to write home about
Although compared to my base,
There are no blackouts
But some don't like my faith
And they want the Blacks out
I guess I have to go.
PEACE OUT!

I imagined

I imagened
the hullabaloo that paced the nation,
an atmosphere ignited
by sparks from the nozzles of guns,
the fear that swirled
in the humid air of tears,
splattered bloods
that decorated the street,
kids longing for a mother to cling to,
mournful hearts and punctured souls,
hopes that went down with the sun,
a beating heart
faster than the bullet that pierced it,
and armors of lifeless bodies.
I imagined chaos.
But my pen
is too plain a utensil
to paint a vivid picture.

Can I talk?

I have been told to speak loud
But I doubt my thoughts would ring through
For I know your wish won't come true
And I know you won't agree.
So, this is meant for the few.

I know birds do sweat
But their feathers block your sight
Because everybody does something
Does not make it right
I've got hope
But I'm not hopeful
I pray for the insincere
And advice the dumb
I send my condolences
To the victims whose pains are numb
Hoodlums with placards
Led by fathers of bastards
Looters & rascals
Bunch of vandals
Chaps without a conscience
Leading votes of no confidence
Against the government whose members
Are our fathers, uncles, friends, and neighbors
They wreak havoc on the soil
They go to war just for its spoils

I don't hear no message, boys
Yet, loud and clear I heard your voice

Oh! Negro!

Oh! Negro!
You've known betrayal like a brother
You've conquered fields and rivers

You've planted seeds and fought wars
You made it all the way across

You surprised your enemies
You survived by any means

You wore the scar
Of a war fought afar

So, when they poke at scars from past wars
Remember that scars are rarely sores
They only remind you of past gores

They would tell you some tale
About how you were born to fail

They would look down on you
But never look up to them

They would trick you off your track
Then stab you in the back

They would put you down and low
But like a seed you always grow
Oh! Negro!

Broken English

You came with your guns and book
And we took your words for gospel

In the land of kings,
the queen's tongue must reign

We brought your language home
and raised it like our own

We took it as a token,
but to our tongues it won't submit.

I'm sorry your darling looks broken.
That bastard couldn't take the heat.

VIII

Places

Poetic city

I'm a poetic city
A receptacle of old ghetto stories
My scenery is straight from the movies
I'm the home for the homeless
I've seen dreams become nightmares
My offspring built this nation
I'm not historic
I am history
The feet of your fathers cleared my path
My dwellers are fighters
Those who leave, survivors
I was the home of shackled arms
Now I'm home to shackled minds
They call me the city of neighborhoods
I'm the city to many hoods
My streets are rugged
My walls, ancient
My colonial past gave out a monumental present
My ambience can be romantic
My accent, mid Atlantic
I'm home to many lakes
I feed Chesapeake
I'm the forgotten city
Forgotten are those with me
Single moms at old malls
With crying babies that play balls

Street soldiers that own guns
I've seen days of protest
And night so grotesque
That make old souls shed tears
Pangs of pain from bangs of gun blaze
Shattered dreams behind a broken window
A dumb youth with a swollen ego
Sought refuge in highness
Made moves in darkness
Oh! No! I'm not perfect
I'm just a city that never rejects
I am Baltimore.
Welcome!

I think I'm Philly

Although my love is so brotherly
I'm home to warriors
No invaders could bother me
I'm sweet:
I've got cuisines named after me

I'm a city that loves back
'cause what you give is what you get
So, I've got no love for those who disrespect
I got a reputation to protect
That's my definition of success

In case you don't know already,
I think I'm Philly
Google me.

The city of wisdom

A city that runs on water
yet runs from water
Boys don't count your bridges
Men are here for riches

Titles don't pay bills
They can take their capital
You house hustlers
You cap it all

Your shops don't fear your roads
As seas smile at the surviving abodes
You inspire harmony in chaos
Strangers will never understand Lagos.

City life

What's there to like in a city?
Is it the expensive meals,
sight that kills,
air that stinks of weed,
or parking that needs a permit?

What's there to like in a city?
Is it the high crime rate,
jewelry so fake,
driving so reckless,
or homie hating the homeless?

What's there to like in a city?
I really can't see.

IX

Nature & twinkles

I'm a survivor

I'm in a place where
Tasteless salt falls from the sky
A place with seasonless rains
Where sometimes
The sun is but a mirage
And other times shade of the tree
Can't save you from its torment
I've witnessed three seasons in a day
I'm a survivor in a way

What am I?

I'm a beauty to the eye
Few of me is beautiful
Few more me is not so fine
I'm a necessary evil

I decorate a city
I shut down towns
I don't show pity
I cover mounts

I'm a blessing from the sky
I show: I don't tell
What, in the world, I'm I?
I'm that snow that fell

Lion king

The sea could beat its chest at the sky
But the moon, the sun, and the stars
Are not bothered by the huff and puff of its tides

Pigs could snort and boars could grumble
Parrots could talk and snakes could rattle
But a sleeping lion is still the king in the jungle

You're beautiful

It shines when you smile
It rains when you cry
I see the smog as you sigh
You house the moon so high

You're littered with the stars
How can you despair
When rainbows are your scars

If you're this awesome,
How beautiful is the One
Who made you what you are?

Tornado

I'm the dancing monster
That sweep shelters off their feet
Nobody dares to bother
To look into the eye of the beast

I mingle with lightning
But I don't strike; I encompass
I tangle with rain
But I don't fall; I land

I'm a spectacle
As I stamp my feet on the ground
I waltz and scuttle
I spiral around and around

I cow the brave
Only fools would wait
Why should I besiege
When I could just...invade

I raid cities
I storm buildings
I've made no friend or enemy
Other plagues envy me

I spew shurikens. I choose
the weapons that I wield
How can I ever lose
When I pick the battlefield?

I steal your dreams
To bury your hopes
I see the grims
As I destroy your homes

I'm world famous
I never lose a clash
I thrive in chaos
I take lives in a flash

I'm just a message
So please don't blame me
But if I could cause this much damage
Fear the one who sent me.

You're a riddle

Your beginning ends my night
Your end begins my day
You do better without light
You make rebels pay

Your innocence clouds your might
Your essence has a say
You bring me down without a fight
You never miss a day

Sleep.

Author's contact:

suleiman.adeyemi@yahoo.com